Zeitgeist 2
Edexcel

Self Study Guide

Clare Parker

OXFORD
UNIVERSITY PRESS

OXFORD
UNIVERSITY PRESS

Great Clarendon Street, Oxford OX2 6DP

Oxford University Press is a department of the University of Oxford.
It furthers the University's objective of excellence in research, scholarship,
and education by publishing worldwide in

Oxford   New York

Auckland   Cape Town   Dar es Salaam   Hong Kong   Karachi
Kuala Lumpur   Madrid   Melbourne   Mexico City   Nairobi
New Delhi   Shanghai   Taipei   Toronto

With offices in

Argentina   Austria   Brazil   Chile   Czech Republic   France   Greece
Guatemala   Hungary   Italy   Japan   South Korea   Poland   Portugal
Singapore   Switzerland   Thailand   Turkey   Ukraine   Vietnam

Oxford is a registered trade mark of Oxford University Press
in the UK and in certain other countries

British Library Cataloguing in Publication Data

Data available

ISBN 978 019 915402 9

3 5 7 9 10 8 6 4 2

Typeset by PDQ Digital Media Solutions Ltd.
Printed in Great Britain by Ashford Colour Press Ltd.

Acknowledgements

The author and publisher would like to thank Melissa Weir (project
manager), Deborah Manning (editor), and Marion Dill (language
consultant).

Contents

General Exam Tips

Here's a reminder of the topics from the Edexcel A2 specification which you need to revise for the examination.

Youth culture and concerns

Lifestyle: health and fitness

The world around us: travel, tourism, environmental issues and the German-speaking world

Education and employment

Customs, traditions, beliefs and religions

National and international events: past, present and future

Literature and the arts

You will be taking two examinations. (Remember that your AS grade represents 50% of your A Level.)

Unit 3: Understanding and Spoken Response in German

The Speaking Test is worth $17\frac{1}{2}$ % of your A Level. The test lasts 11–13 minutes. There is only one task: presenting any issue of your choice to the examiner in German, taking a clear stance on it, discussing it with the examiner and moving on to discuss other issues.

Unit 4: Research, Understanding and Written Response in German

This paper is worth $32\frac{1}{2}$ % of your A Level. The time allowed is two hours and 30 minutes. There are three sections:

Section A: Translating a short passage of English into German
Section B: Writing either a creative essay or a discursive essay of 240–270 words
Section C: Writing a research-based essay of 240–270 words.

For the research-based essay you have to choose a topic from one of the following areas:

Ein deutschsprachiges Gebiet – Ein historischer Zeitraum – Aspekte der heutigen deutschen Gesellschaft – Deutsche Literatur und Kunst

There is more information on the Unit 3 exam starting on page 8 and more information on the Unit 4 exam starting on page 14.

Pass grades for this examination range from A* and A down to E.

The descriptions of what you need to be able to do are very similar to those at AS Level, **but remember that this is in the context of the more demanding texts and tasks which you will meet at A2.** Two new things which are expected are an ability to translate from and into German accurately and an ability to cope with the unpredictable when you are talking to someone. Here's a reminder of the other expectations:

If you pass A Level German with an A grade, it means you can:

> ▸ clearly understand spoken language, including details and opinions.

> ▸ work out what someone is trying to say even if they don't spell it out in detail.

> ▸ clearly understand written texts, understanding both the gist and the details

> ▸ talk fluently, giving your opinions and justifying them, and using a good range of vocabulary and generally accurate pronunciation and word order.

> ▸ organise your ideas and write them up well in German.

> ▸ write using a wide range of vocabulary and grammatical structures without making many mistakes.

If you pass A Level German with an E grade, it means you:

> ▸ show some understanding of spoken German, even if you have difficulties when the language is complex and miss some of the details.

> ▸ can sometimes work out what someone is trying to say even if they don't give all the details.

> ▸ understand straightforward written texts, although you don't always understand more difficult writing.

> ▸ can speak in German, and convey basic information, perhaps a little hesitantly and relying on material you have learned by heart. There is probably some English influence on your pronunciation.

> ▸ can convey information in writing, perhaps with some difficulty in organising your material and expressing it.

> ▸ use a range of vocabulary and structures, but quite often you make mistakes.

Preparing for the exams

You can see from these lists that when planning your revision there are really five areas you need to practise:

Speaking – Reading and research – Writing – Vocabulary – Grammar

There are tips on how to prepare each area overleaf.

How to revise

Speaking

- ▸ Take every opportunity to practise speaking German – in lessons, with the language assistant, with a friend, with anyone you know who speaks German.

- ▸ Keep researching the topic you have chosen for your oral exam, noting both facts and useful vocabulary and expressions. Choose a topic you are interested in and then decide on a definite stance you want to take, arguing that some aspect is or is not a good thing, for example.

- ▸ Record some of your ideas, then listen to them to see what areas still need practice – perhaps fluency, pronunciation, word order or good use of vocabulary and structures.

Reading and research

- ▸ You need to read widely in order to research your chosen oral topic and also the material for your research-based essay.

- ▸ Once you have chosen an oral topic, read a good variety of texts in German on it, looking for a suitable 'angle' to present to the examiner. Once you are clear what you want to focus on, re-read everything of relevance, making notes on useful facts and ideas, but also of vocabulary which will help you express them.

- ▸ Adopt a similar approach to the reading for your research-based essay, collecting relevant articles and making notes in sections. For example, if you are studying a book, you should make notes on each of the main characters, on the themes, perhaps a short biography of the author and so on.

- ▸ If you want to improve your general reading ability in German, try magazines, material on the internet which interests you or a 'dual-language' reading book, where you get the original German on one page and an English translation on the opposite one. This is an excellent way to practise reading longer texts without losing heart!

Writing

- ▸ Write out the basic facts for each aspect of the cultural topics you have studied and learn them.

- ▸ Practise planning essay questions, both creative/discursive and research-based. Jot down ideas for each paragraph – in German – along with key vocabulary.

- ▸ Look carefully at marked work and identify what grammar errors you are making. Then check them in a grammar book and try some practice exercises.

- ▸ Make sure you are writing – and learning – lists of key vocabulary for each aspect of your researched topic. In addition, learn a good range of 'essay phrases' for introducing ideas, giving opinions, summing up and so on.

Vocabulary

▶ Learn lists of words regularly and build in time to go back over words you learned a week or two ago. Reinforcement makes them stick!

▶ Choose a system of recording new words which works for you. It could be paper lists, sticky notes round the mirror, small sections on individual cards, index cards with German on one side and English meaning on the other, recording the German words and their English meanings on tape, making posters to stick on your bedroom wall ... what's important is that you are noting the words and going over them regularly.

▶ Go back over previous essays, highlighting good words and phrases and writing the English in the margin, then use this to test yourself. Words are often easier to learn in context.

Grammar

▶ Keep doing practice exercises in areas where you know you are weak.

▶ Use reading texts to practise thinking grammatically. For example, highlight a selection of adjectives, then write out the English for the phrases in which they appear. Test yourself by reproducing the German phrases accurately, complete with all the correct agreements!

▶ Keep thinking about word order. Analyse sentences regularly, looking at the position of the verb (past participle if appropriate). Is the **Time –Manner – Place** rule being applied at all times?

▶ Keep learning from your verb tables until you know all the forms of each tense of regular verbs and the most common irregular verbs. Test yourself using a die. 1 = *ich*, 2 = *du*, 3 = *er/sie/es*, 4 = *wir*, 5 = *ihr*, 6 = *sie/Sie*. Use a verb list, choose an infinitive and a tense at random, throw the die and say the correct form of the verb. Practise until you can do it without hesitation.

Getting the timing right

▶ Worthwhile revision is often a question of timing. Some things need to be done as you go along and can't be left until the week before the exam. You should set regular time aside for learning and re-visiting your vocabulary lists and keep refining your knowledge of grammar. Regular speaking practice is a must – you can't make a lot of progress in the last few days.

▶ So what can you do at the last minute? Keep your confidence up by going over vocabulary lists you have already revised, by reading through good essays you have written and perhaps writing plans for questions you haven't written up in full. In short, you should feel that you have already done all the important things and just need to keep everything ticking over.

Speaking

The Speaking Test: what you need to know
Your task is to present an issue and take a definite stance on it.

Timing

The test will last 11–13 minutes and is divided into three sections:

- ▶ 1 minute: you outline the issue you have chosen and explain your stance on it.
- ▶ 4 minutes: the examiner will challenge you to defend your point of view, asking you questions and taking the opposite viewpoint.
- ▶ 6–8 minutes: the examiner will then introduce a minimum of two other unpredictable areas to discuss. These issues may or may not relate to your chosen issue, but it will be a general discussion in which you will not be required to show particular factual knowledge or knowledge of German-language culture. The aim is to assess your speaking skills.

How the Speaking Test is marked

The test is marked out of 50, with marks given for four different aspects:

- ▶ *Response* (20 marks)
  This rewards your ability to respond spontaneously and well to what you are asked, showing an impressive range of vocabulary and grammatical structures.
- ▶ *Quality of Response* (7 marks)
  To do well here, you need to speak accurately, with very good pronunciation and intonation.
- ▶ *Reading and research* (7 marks)
  You need to show evidence of in-depth research into your chosen topic and, when you are discussing the unexpected topics, of wide reading generally.
- ▶ *Comprehension and development* (16 marks)
  You need to show a good understanding of what you are asked, even when the questions are complex or challenging. You need to be able to develop your answers, giving examples and evidence to back up your opinions.

What makes a good topic? Something you are interested in and have views about! It can be, but doesn't have to be, in a German context, but you need to have read widely on the topic in German in order to have the vocabulary to be able to discuss it well. Here are three possible ideas of topics and stances:

- ▶ Atomenergie – die einzige Lösung für unseren zukünftigen Energiebedarf
- ▶ Das Abitur – abwechslungsreicher, detaillierter und interessanter als unser A Level
- ▶ Die Filme von Fassbinder – heutzutage noch immer bedeutend

Planning your topic

The presentation

You have only one minute in which to introduce your topic and present the stance you want to take on it, so you need to be very clear about what you are trying to say. You will probably want to write your presentation out and then learn it and should use no more than 150–170 words in total. Time it to make sure it lasts about a minute. You need to state what your topic is, explain the stance you want to take on it and give some general reasons. Remember that the examiner will come back to the points you make and challenge you on them, so make sure you have your justifications ready. Useful phrases for this section include:

> *Ich habe dieses Thema ausgewählt, weil ...*
> *Meiner Meinung nach, ...*
> *Ich bin der Meinung, dass. ...*
> *Ich finde, dass ...*
> *Ich habe mehrere Gründe, zum Beispiel ...*
> *Warum? Ganz einfach, weil ...*

Of course, research and a good knowledge of your topic are vital. There isn't room to show off everything you know in the initial presentation, but you should mention there the things you will be happy to come back to. For each aspect you mention, you need to prepare a set of well-organised notes. Write the key facts for each and learn them: you won't be asked to recite them, but you will be able to slip them in as examples to illustrate the points you are making. Knowing your material really well will give you the confidence to speak fluently.

You know that the examiner is going to challenge your views. Try to predict what s/he might ask and then decide what you are going to say in response. There is more information on this aspect on page 10.

Once everything is planned, you just need to practise. Make a note of the questions you are asked in practice sessions with your teacher or the assistant, so that you gradually build up a list of things you can answer well. You can practise on your own by using these questions and recording your responses. Listen to them with the Edexcel mark scheme in front of you and analyse how you are doing.

Defending your case

The examiner will challenge your views. This is not an exercise which requires you to balance both sides of an argument. You must stick to your initial argument and defend it. You need to have two things ready:

▸ a list of reasons why you think what you do

▸ an idea of all the arguments the examiner might use to argue against you and – this is important – points you can make against each of them.

Imagine you have decided to argue in favour of renewable sources of energy. Notes on your arguments might include:

▸ Es ist eine Lösung, die uns erlaubt, weniger andere Ressourcen zu benutzen und damit die Erde zu schützen.

▸ Atomenergie ist zu gefährlich – es gibt zu viele Unfallrisiken, Probleme mit Atommüllentsorgung oder Entsorgung der alten Atomkraftwerke.

▸ Es ist zweifellos eine Lösung, aber nach dem aktuellen Stand der Wissenschaft gibt es noch andere Möglichkeiten für die Zukunft.

The examiner might use some of the following arguments. Decide what you would say to counter each one, then compare your ideas with those printed upside down below.

1. Glauben Sie, es ist realistisch, die notwendige Energie von erneuerbaren Quellen zu bekommen?

2. Wie funktioniert beispielsweise Sonnen- und Windenergie bei Autos?

3. Unser Energiebedarf wird immer mehr steigen. Glauben Sie, dass es genug Energie geben wird, wenn wir uns nur auf erneuerbare Quellen verlassen?

zu Fuß gehen oder ganz einfach die Heizung etwas herunterdrehen.
Beispiel nicht so oft mit dem Auto fahren, mehr mit dem Fahrrad fahren, mehr
viel Energie und müssen daher lernen, unseren Verbrauch zu begrenzen: zum
3. Ich glaube, wir sollten unsere Einstellung ändern. Wir benutzen schon viel zu

Wasser produzieren kann.
betreiben lassen. Es kommt darauf an, ob man mehr Energie von Wind und
weiterhin Fahrzeuge produzieren wird, die sich mit anderen Energiequellen
2. Es gibt schon Autos, die mit Elektrizität fahren. Es ist also möglich, dass man

hat schon in den letzten zehn Jahren große Fortschritte gemacht.
neue Technologien wird es vielleicht in der Zukunft möglich sein, ... zu ... Man
1. Derzeit scheint es nicht sehr realistisch zu sein, aber durch Forschung und

Read and listen to this student defending his argument (CD track 2). His topic is crime and he has taken the stance that prison and tough penalties are the only way to combat crime. This is the section of the oral where the examiner begins to challenge his views.

E: Die meisten Kriminellen begehen noch weitere Verbrechen, wenn sie aus dem Gefängnis kommen. Bedeutet das nicht, dass Gefängnisse sinnlos sind?

S: Nein, dem stimme ich nicht zu. Ohne Furcht vor Haftstrafen wird es viel mehr Verbrechen geben. Da bin ich sicher. Wenn ein Krimineller nach einer Haftstrafe wieder Verbrechen begeht, könnte man sagen, dass der Gefängnisaufenthalt zu bequem und einfach war. Haftstrafen sollten länger und viel unbequemer sein.

E: Muss man also nicht jeden Kriminellen nach seinem ersten Verbrechen ins Gefängnis schicken?

S: Nein, das habe ich nicht gemeint. Wichtig ist, dass jeder, der gegen das Gesetz verstößt, weiß, dass er sein Verbrechen irgendwie wieder gutmachen muss. Wenn ein Jugendlicher beispielsweise einige Tage damit verbringen müsste, die Straßen zu reinigen, würde er lernen, dass sein Benehmen unangenehme Folgen gehabt hat. Vielleicht würde er dann nachdenken, bevor er wieder ein Verbrechen begeht.

E: Glauben Sie nicht, dass es Fälle gibt, wo es besser wäre, einfach mit den jungen Kriminellen zu sprechen und ihnen zu erklären, dass das, was sie gemacht haben, nicht in Ordnung ist?

S: Im Gegenteil. Ich bin der Meinung, dass solche Kriminellen uns auslachen. Wie werden sie ihr Benehmen ändern, wenn sie keine Strafe bekommen? Man muss ihnen zeigen und nicht nur sagen, dass Verbrechen nicht in Ordnung sind. Sonst machen sie das immer wieder, davon bin ich überzeugt.

Learn some useful phrases for disagreeing (politely!) with the examiner. Examples include:

Nein, im Gegenteil. Ich glaube, dass, …

Ich bin überhaupt nicht der gleichen Meinung, weil …

Meiner Meinung nach ist das nicht richtig, weil …

Es stimmt nicht, dass …

Ja, vielleicht, aber man darf nicht vergessen, dass …..

The last 6–8 minutes of the oral will be a spontaneous discussion on at least two unpredictable areas. These may – or may not – relate to the topic you chose to talk about. It is worth making a list of possible areas which lead on from your topic, because the examiner may well start with one of those. Advice on this is given below. See page 13 for information about other topics which might come up in this section.

For example, if your topic was tourism and you argued that tourism is always bad for the environment, the examiner might decide to move onto other environmental issues or to something related to travel and tourism. Possible questions include:

▶ Für welche anderen Aspekte der Umwelt interessieren Sie sich?

▶ Was tun Sie persönlich für die Umwelt?

▶ Glauben Sie, dass man heutzutage zu viel über die Umwelt redet?

▶ Welche Vorteile hat Tourismus für ein Urlaubsgebiet?

▶ Welche Gebiete in Deutschland kennen Sie?

▶ Gefällt es Ihnen, Tourist zu sein, oder wohnen Sie lieber langfristig im Ausland?

▶ Hoffen Sie, in der Zukunft viel zu reisen? Warum (nicht)?

Look at these possible topics and stances and for each one think up three questions the examiner might ask in order to move the conversation on to a different topic. Then compare your answers with those printed upside down below.

1. Man redet zu viel über gesundes Essen. Wenn man genug Sport treibt, kann man essen, was man will.

2. Kultur ist etwas für die ältere Generation und bedeutet Jugendlichen nichts.

3. Fünf Jahre auf derselben Arbeitsstelle ist schon viel zu lang.

> Do the same for your own topic. Write a list of possible opening questions on related topics and practise answering them. You can't guarantee they will come up, but there's a reasonable chance.

Wie finden Sie das?
▶ In Deutschland kann man im Alter von 28 immer noch auf der Universität sein.
▶ Warum sind junge Leute zwischen 18 und 25 arbeitslos ?
▶ Was wäre für Sie der ideale Job?

3

▶ Was wäre für Sie eine sinnvolle Rente?
▶ Was sollte man machen, um junge Musiker zu fördern?
▶ Wer ist Ihr Lieblingsautor und warum?

2

▶ Bietet Ihre Schule genug Sport an?
▶ Verdienen berühmte Sportler zu viel?
▶ Was ist schlimmer für die Gesundheit – Alkohol oder Tabak?

1

Other topics which could crop up in the last part of the speaking test are those listed in the specification. Here are a few sample questions as examples of what you might be asked. You can listen to students answering some of them on the CD (track 3) and find a transcript in a word document on the CD ROM.

Youth culture and concerns

▶ Wie sieht die Kultur der heutigen jungen Leute aus?

▶ Wer sind die Vorbilder für junge Leute?

▶ Was sind die Hauptgründe für Jugendkriminalität?

Lifestyle: health and fitness

▶ Glauben Sie, dass man heutzutage zu viel über Gesundheit redet?

▶ Um welche Aspekte der Gesundheit kümmern Sie sich am meisten?

▶ Könnte man sagen, dass unsere Gesellschaft noch nie so ungesund war?

The world around us: travel, tourism, environmental issues and the German-speaking world

▶ Reisen bedeutet auch Lernen. Stimmen Sie zu?

▶ Bringt der Tourismus mehr Nachteile als Vorteile?

▶ Was muss man machen, um mit sehr wenig Energiebedarf zu leben?

▶ Welche Aspekte der Umwelt sind für Sie am wichtigsten?

Education and employment

▶ Wie bewerten Sie Ihre Ausbildung?

▶ Sollte man junge Leute fördern, eine Weiterbildung zu machen?

▶ Welche Auskwirkungen auf die Gesellschaft hat Arbeitslosigkeit im Allgemeinen?

Customs, traditions, beliefs and religions

▶ Welche Traditionen sind für Sie wichtig?

▶ Wie wichtig ist der Glaube in der heutigen Gesellschaft?

National and international events: past, present and future

▶ Was kann man lernen, wenn man Geschichte studiert?

▶ Lohnt es sich, wählen zu gehen?

▶ Wird es immer Kriege geben?

Literature and the arts

▶ Erzählen Sie etwas über ein Buch/einen Film, das/der Sie sehr beeinflusst hat!

▶ Wenn Sie ein Kulturfest veranstalten müssten, was wären Ihre Hauptziele?

Research, Understanding and Written Response Unit

This unit takes two hours and 30 minutes. There are three sections and they will all be linked to the topic list on page 4. You can plan your time as you wish, but it might be best to allow at least an hour for each of the two essays, which would leave up to half an hour to spend on Section A.

Section A (10 marks)

A short passage of about 80 words of English which you have to translate into German.

Section B (45 marks)

Either: a discursive essay of between 240 and 270 words. This type of essay requires you to argue a point, balance the pros and cons of an argument or give your opinion on a topic and justify it.

Or: a creative essay of 240–270 words. You may be asked to write the story behind a photograph or document, to continue a story opening which you are given or to produce some other form of imaginary writing.

Section C (45 marks)

A research-based essay. There will be one question on each of the research-based topic areas:

Ein deutschsprachiges Gebiet
Ein historischer Zeitraum
Aspekte der heutigen deutschen Gesellschaft
Deutsche Literatur und Kunst

You choose one title and write an essay of 240–270 words.

The key ways to prepare are by:

▸ doing plenty of practice of translation into German, revising vocabulary and grammar points as you go.

▸ practising writing creative or discursive essays (240–270 words) on each of the general topic areas listed on page 4.

▸ choosing a research topic which really interests you, discussing the areas you plan to focus on with your teacher and researching it, making careful notes on the different aspects as you go. Then you need to write practice essays of 240–270 words.

▸ working through the exam-type questions and tips on the following pages.

Section A

Übersetzen Sie die folgenden Sätze auf Deutsch:

a Nowadays petrol is becoming more and more expensive.

b We should encourage people to leave their car at home.

c Fast cars are exciting but they waste a lot of energy.

d We could also do something for the environment by not flying very often.

e If you spend your ideal holiday at the beach, find a beach near you!

f Although we understand the problem, we do not want to do anything about it.

g No-one knows what will happen in the future.

> Think grammatically! Which sentence or sentences require you to use each of the following? Work it out, then check the answers which are printed upside down.
>
> **i** the construction *indem* followed by a relative clause
> **ii** a *wenn* clause
> **iii** a modal verb
> **iv** an adjective which will need agreement
> **v** a negative construction
> **vi** a comparative
> **vii** a subordinate clause
> **viii** a verb in the future tense
> **ix** a construction using *man*
>
> **i** d   **ii** e   **iii** b,d,f   **iv** c,e   **v** a   **vi** a   **vii** b,d,e,f,g   **viii** g   **ix** b

> Remember that you can't always translate word for word – for example, 'near you' is best translated by six words, not two.

> Check everything very carefully. Is every verb in the correct tense and does it agree with its subject? Does every adjective which needs agreement have it?

g Keiner weiß, was in der Zukunft passieren wird.

f Obwohl wir das Problem gut verstehen können, wollen wir nichts dagegen machen.

e Wenn Sie Ihren idealen Urlaub am Strand verbringen, finden Sie einen Strand in der Nähe von zu Hause!

d Wir können auch etwas für die Umwelt tun, indem wir nicht so oft mit dem Flugzeug fliegen.

c Schnelle Autos sind aufregend, aber sie verbrauchen viel Energie.

b Man sollte alle Leute anregen, ihre Autos zu Hause zu lassen.

a Heutzutage wird das Benzin immer teurer.

Section A

Translate into German:

We must all try not to waste the earth's resources. Everyone can do something for the environment, by turning down the heating or switching lights off when leaving the room. But is that enough?

Young people need to accept that we will no longer be able to drive everywhere as we used to. Anyone who has bought a car should leave it in the garage as often as possible. Car-sharing is one solution and allows you to save money and to pollute the atmosphere less.

Most people could do better. We know it's irresponsible to buy goods with lots of packaging or to live on ready meals. We ought to make a little more effort.

> Always try to spot the 'grammar tricks' the examiner has planted in the English passage. To translate the first paragraph well, you need to remember to translate 'by' with *indem* followed by the present tense of the German verb to translate the English present participle forms 'switching off' and 'turning down'.

> Be especially careful over the spelling of words which are similar to, but not quite the same as, their English equivalents. In this passage, words like this include the translations of 'atmosphere' and 'accept'. Use your dictionary well – how do you translate 'resources' and 'car-sharing'?

> When checking your translation, look carefully at the verb forms. Have you got the right constructions to translate some of the English phrases? Do you need *zu* plus the infititive in some places? Have you correctly translated the perfect tense needed in the second paragraph? Have you used the correct modal verb and in the correct tense?

Suggested translation

Jeder sollte versuchen, die Bodenschätze nicht zu verschwenden. Jeder kann etwas für die Umwelt tun, indem er die Heizung herunterdreht oder das Licht ausmacht, wenn er aus dem Zimmer geht. Aber reicht das?

Junge Leute müssen akzeptieren, dass wir nicht mehr überall mit dem Auto hinfahren können, wie wir das immer gemacht haben. Wer ein Auto gekauft hat, sollte es so oft wie möglich in der Garage lassen. Fahrgemeinschaften sind eine mögliche Lösung und erlauben uns, Benzin zu sparen und die Atmosphäre weniger zu belasten.

Die meisten Leute könnten es besser machen. Wir wissen, dass es nicht vernünftig ist, Produkte mit viel Verpackung zu kaufen oder uns nur von Fertiggerichten zu ernähren. Wir sollten uns ein bisschen mehr Mühe machen.

Section B   Essay writing

Good essay writing is really the key to this paper, as it is worth 90% of the marks! Whichever sort of essay you are writing, there are three vital stages: planning, writing and checking and you need to find time for all three, even under exam conditions.

Planning

Don't rush this stage. 5–10 minutes thinking about the question, deciding on your argument and dividing it into paragraphs, jotting down the facts you want to use and thinking out a good introduction and conclusion is time very well spent. Keep referring to the title to make sure every paragraph is relevant to the question. You might also note vocabulary and phrases you want to use in each paragraph. Then, when everything is in order, start writing, and make sure you stick to the plan.

Writing

Work through your notes for each paragraph. Write them up using a variety of sentence lengths, interesting vocabulary and a range of grammatical constructions. Be especially careful about the links between the paragraphs, so the examiner can follow the argument easily. See the ideas on page 23.

Checking

Read your essay once through to check the flow of ideas and make sure each sentence makes sense. Then do a more detailed check, looking especially for these common errors:

- ▶ verbs which don't agree with their subject or are in the wrong tense
- ▶ adjectives which don't match the noun they describe
- ▶ phrases which are not idiomatic and don't sound German
- ▶ misspellings, especially of words similar to, but not the same as, English
- ▶ missing umlauts
- ▶ word order, especially subordinate clauses.

It is also useful to practise planning essays, even if you don't write them up in full. Writing well-thought-out plans for possible essay titles is excellent revision in itself, and gives you some material to look over in the last revision periods before the exam.

Make some useful revision notes by copying out sentences from your essays which had mistakes in them and then putting in the corrections in a different colour. Doing this will remind you of errors you have made and – even more importantly – remind you how to correct them.

Section B
Structuring your essay

Obviously, your essay needs a beginning, a middle and an end, but there are different ways to plan it. Here are a few possibilities:

▶ **For and against**

This is the classic 'balanced argument' technique where you write one or two paragraphs in favour of something, then one or two more against it and then conclude with your personal opinion.

▶ **Tennis match**

This is another useful way to structure an essay in which you want to put forward both sides of an argument. Each paragraph is used to put forward a point from one side of the argument, then give the reasons against it. It is useful if you want to put one side of the argument over strongly; each paragraph gives a reason for your argument, then explains why those opposed to it are wrong. The essay needs to end with a strong conclusion.

▶ Chronological

A chronological approach is suitable for certain types of question. An essay about plot development in a film or a novel can follow this pattern, as long as you careful not to lapse into just re-telling the story. You may want to describe a character at the beginning of the story, refer to events which happen and the effect it has on him or her and then conclude by saying how he or she has changed. It could also be a useful approach for an essay on, say, the impact of tourism in a particular region, if you wanted to explain how the industry has developed over time.

▶ Build the argument

Some essays practically plan themselves! If you want to write about the way cinematic techniques contribute to plot development in a film, you may decide that the relevant points are sound, lighting, the use of flashbacks and the range of camera angles used. So it makes sense to devote one paragraph to each of those, making each point clear by giving examples and then saying what the effect of each is. Top and tail this with an introduction and conclusion (see page 23) and you have a perfect plan.

> Make a point of using different styles of essay plan in the practice essays you write so you become familiar with the possibilities and see what works best in each particular set of circumstances.

Research, Understanding and Written Response Unit

The essay: making your points

▸ **The beginning**

Your introduction needs to set the scene. It should pose the question you will be answering, but not give away your conclusion. Look at these notes for possible introductions for particular titles.

Analysieren Sie die Rolle der Musik im Film ‚Lola rennt‘.

‚Lola rennt‘ findet im heutigen Berlin statt, und es ist ein Film voller Energie. Ich werde erklären, warum dieser Film wenig Text, aber viel Aktion und Musik hat. Ich möchte deutlich machen, was der Regisseur damit sagen will.

Berlin ist eine Großstadt voller Geschichte, aber sie ist auch ein Symbol für die moderne Welt. Analysieren Sie diese Ideen und Gegensätze.

Berlin ist eine eigenartige Stadt mit einer besonderen Geschichte. Ich möchte hier ihre Geschichte und ihre Wende von einer geteilten Stadt zum modernen Symbol erforschen. Ich hoffe dabei, ihre Geschichte, ihr Architektur und ihre Leute ein bisschen zu erklären.

▸ **The middle**

Stick to the paragraph plan you have worked out. Make it easy for the examiner to follow your argument by 'signposting' it, giving an idea at the beginning of each new paragraph of what point you are going to make and how it follows on from the previous paragraph. Is it another point in the same argument or does it contradict your previous point?

Adding a new argument:

Das führt dazu, dass ...	That leads to ...
Die Folge ist, dass ...	The consequence is that ...
Wir müssen nicht vergessen, dass ...	We must not forget that ...
Was ich eigentlich sagen wollte, ist ...	What I really meant was ....
Außerdem	Moreover
Übrigens	Incidentally/By the way

Contradicting your previous point:

Im Gegenteil	On the contrary
Auf der einen Seite/Auf der anderen Seite	On the one hand/On the other hand
In Wirklichkeit	In reality
Es ist fraglich, ob ...	It's questionable whether ...
Das hat damit nichts zu tun	That has nothing to do with it
Es kann sein, dass ...	It may be true that ...

▸ **The end**

The conclusion is the place to answer the question and to give your personal viewpoint, which should arise logically out of the arguments you have put forward. Useful phrases include:

Ich bin davon überzeugt, dass ...	I am convinced that ...
im Großen und Ganzen	on the whole
zum Schluss	in conclusion
kurz gesagt	in short
ohne Zweifel	undeniably
alles in allem	all things considered

Section B   Writing a creative essay

What you have to do

A stimulus is provided and you are asked to write an imaginative response to it. The stimulus could be a photo or cartoon, for which you are asked to imagine how the situation came about or perhaps predict what might happen next. The stimulus could also be a text, perhaps a diary extract or other piece of writing which you are asked to respond to or continue in your own words.

Typical questions

1

Erzählen Sie die Geschichte von diesen jungen Leuten.

2 Setzen Sie diese Geschichte fort und benutzten Sie die Verben im Perfekt und Imperfekt.

Das erste Mal, das ich Heinrich gesehen habe, war er sehr betrübt. Seine Kleider waren schmutzig und zerrissen und seine Augen waren rot. Seine Hände und Gesicht waren auch schmutzig und er sah sehr dünn aus. Er sah mich zweifelnd an und ich ...

3 Schreiben Sie den Artikel, der diesen Titel folgt!

Diese zwei Jugendlichen haben gerade ihren Traumurlaub gewonnen!

> Some teachers don't prepare their classes for this type of essay, but concentrate on practising discursive essays. If that is the case, don't try this out in the exam! You need to have had several practice essays marked so that you can see exactly what the requirements are.

How the essay is marked

There are 45 marks in total.

Range and application of language: 10 marks, i.e. a good range of vocabulary and complex structures, well handled.

Accuracy: 5 marks

Understanding and response: 15 marks, i.e. a good understanding of the question and an imaginative response to it.

Organisation and development: 15 marks, i.e. a clear, well-planned piece which is easy to follow and where the ideas are developed.

Section B   Writing a discursive essay

What you have to do

A discursive essay requires you to organise ideas and arguments and build a well-structured answer to a question on a general issue. The information on essay structures on pages 17 and 18 is particularly relevant here.

> Remember that the essay questions will all relate to the general topic areas from the specification, so learning vocabulary for each one will be really useful, as will revising the essays you have written on these topics during the year. Look through your textbook for ideas for other questions on each topic and write plans for them – re-reading them will be useful last minute revision.

Typical questions

1. ‚Heutzutage nehmen viele junge Leute das Leben nicht sehr ernst.‘ Stimmen Sie zu?

2. Glauben Sie, dass die meisten Leute Sport nicht aus Vergnügung, sondern nur für ihre Gesundheit treiben?

3. Warum reist man immer noch in die Ferne, obwohl man so viel von Luftverschmutzung und Planetenkrise hört?

4. Was sollten die Ziele eines Ausbildungssystemes sein?

5. Braucht man noch Gott in der modernen Welt?

6. ‚Um kultiviert zu sein, muss man über nationale und internationale kulturelle Veranstaltungen Bescheid wissen.‘ Stimmt das?

7. Ist es wahr, dass es heutzutage altmodisch ist, sogennante ‚Literatur‘ zu lesen?

> It's important to come up with a wide-ranging answer to the question and to devise separate paragraphs to make your various points. For question 3, for example, you might write first on the merits of travel, and then on how to limit the environmental effects of your journeys before concluding that travel can be useful for learning more about the earth we are trying to protect.

How the essay is marked

There are 45 marks in total.

Three sections are exactly the same as for the creative essay, so check the information on page 20: *range and application of language* (10 marks), *accuracy* (5 marks) and *organisation and development* (15 marks). The remaining 15 marks are for *understanding and response*, which for the discursive essay means that you have fully understood all the implications of the question and answered it well.

Section C   Writing a research-based essay

What you have to do

You need to choose a topic to research from one of the four topic areas listed below and conduct your own research so that you will be able to answer an essay question on it. The questions require you to present relevant aspects of your research and convey your own views and opinions on the topic. The questions will all require answers which analyse and evaluate what you have found out, rather than just stating the facts. Here are ideas of the type of research areas required:

Geographical area (e.g. a region or a city)

Key people and events, issues which affect the area, such as demographic, environmental, economic, social and political factors.

Historical study

A specific period of history relevant to Germany or a German-speaking country, including key people, events and issues.

Aspects of modern German-speaking society

Key current and recent* events, social, political and cultural issues.
*recent means 21st or late 20th century

Literature and the arts

A study of a text, play or film, including its characters, key themes, social and cultural setting and style or techniques.

You need to consult a wide range of source material on the topic you have chosen, because this will give you a broad spectrum of views and lots of useful vocabulary ideas. Of course, the Internet will provide a lot of material, but other sources likely to be relevant include:

Geographical area (e.g. a region or a city)
Material from the relevant tourist board, personal experiences if you have visited the area, interviews with those who know it well.

Historical study
History textbooks, encylopaedias.

Aspects of modern German-speaking society
Newspapers and magazines, online news services, interviews with people from the field, TV and radio programmes.

Literature and the arts
Text or films by the same author or director, critical material, material from the arts sections of newspapers or websites.

> Keep copies or recordings of all the source material you use, so that you can refer to it as you work on your revision notes. When you make notes, list the source of all the facts so that you can find them again if you want to check them or find out more.

Section C   Typical questions

Geographical area

▸ Überlegen Sie sich die geografischen Aspekte Ihrer gewählten Gegend und bewerten Sie ihre Wichtigkeit.

▸ Analysieren Sie die wirtschaftlichen Aspekte Ihrer gewählten Gegend.

Historical study

▸ Analysieren Sie die Ursachen und Auswirkungen eines wichtigen Ereignisses in Ihrem gewählten Zeitraum.

▸ Wählen Sie eine wichtige Person aus dieser Zeit. Was können wir von ihm/ihr lernen?

Aspects of modern German-speaking society

▸ Welcher Aspekt der deutschprachigen Gesellschaft ist für Sie besonders faszinierend?

▸ Wählen Sie einen Aspekt der heutigen deutschsprachigen Gesellschaft. Wie ist die heutige Lage und wie wird die Lage in der Zukunft aussehen?

Literature and the arts

▸ Bewundern Sie den Stil des Autors/des Regisseurs, mit dem Sie sich beschäftigt haben? Warum (nicht)?

▸ Vergleichen Sie zwei Personen in dem Buch/in dem Film, das Sie gelesen/den Sie gesehen haben.

> It is good essay style to weave facts and opinions together, as in this extract on a visit to Berlin today, which makes reference to the history of the city.

Es ist fast unbeschreiblich, was man fühlt, wenn man zu Fuß durch das Brandenburger Tor geht. Ich hatte das Gefühl, als ob ich ein Teil der lebendigen Geschichte sei. Vor der Wende war sowas nicht möglich, da das Brandenburger Tor hinter der Mauer stand. Jetzt ist das Tor ist ein Symbol der Einheit Deutschlands. Wenn man Berlin am 3. Oktober besucht, kann man auch den Tag der deutschen Einheit und damit den Tag des Mauerfalls im Jahr 1989 begehen.

The student who wrote this is evaluating the city of Berlin. S/he is incorporating her/his own feelings about walking through the Brandenburg Gate but in addition s/he has slipped several facts into the paragraph: that the Brandenburg Gate stood behind the Wall, the date of the celebration of German unity and the fact that ceremonies are still held every year in memory of what happened.

How the essay is marked

There are 45 marks in total.

Reading, research and understanding: 30 marks, i.e. clear evidence of extensive, in-depth reading and research.

Organisation and development: 9 marks, i.e. organising your material effectively into a well-planned essay.

Quality of language: 6 marks, i.e. fluent and varied language showing a wide vocabulary, effective word order and a command of a good range of complex structures. Also, a high level of accuracy.

Grammar

All the grammar you learned for AS is still needed, and there are some extra points for A2. Pages 25–31 revise AS grammar, reminding you what you should know and giving you phrases and sentences to translate from and into German for practice. Pages 32–33 revise the points you will be learning on the A2 course, also practised through sentences to translate.

Grammar is even more important at A2 than it was at AS. So, what can you to do make sure you really do know your stuff?

Pay attention when grammar is explained. If you learn the rules and the exceptions and do some practice exercises, you will be surprised how much of it will stick.

Accept that there is quite a lot of detail to master and be prepared to go over things regularly. Re-read your grammar notes, re-do practice exercises, ask questions if you come across things you don't fully understand.

Be pro-active. Go through marked written work, looking carefully at the things which have been corrected. Decide which ones are 'silly mistakes', caused by forgetting things which you know well and make a list of them, so you can try to avoid them in future. Then look for errors where you are not quite sure why it is wrong. Ask, if necessary, then look up that grammar point in the grammar section of your textbook and in the relevant section of the grammar workbook. Keep practising and asking questions until you do understand it. When you understand it, review it by writing grammar notes on it in your own words, adding examples.

Make a list of example sentences from your written work which use some of the more complex grammar points well. Learn them, and use them as models for other sentences with different vocabulary but which use the same basic structure. Make a point of including a good variety of grammatical structures in the practice essays you write.

Work through the exercises on the following pages. If there are practice sentences you find hard to translate, learn the correct version from the answer section by heart.

Revision of AS Grammar: nouns, adjectives, adverbs

Check the grammar section of *Zeitgeist 2* and/or the Grammar Workbook if you need to know more about any of these things:

▶ typical masculine endings for nouns, such as *-ant, -er, -ich, -ig, -ing, -ismus,* etc

▶ typical feminine endings for nouns, such as *-e, -heit, -ik, -in, keit, -schaft, -ung,* etc

▶ typical neuter endings for nouns, such as *-chen, -lein, -um,* etc

▶ how to form the plurals of nouns – is it *-n, -en, -nen, -s, -er* and does it have an umlaut? Or does it require a plural at all?

▶ how to make adjectives agree in number and case

▶ forming possessive adjectives like *mein, dein, sein, ihr, unser,* etc

▶ using *kein* with appropriate endings to translate the negative

▶ using adjectives as adverbs

▶ comparing adjectives by adding *-er* plus the appropriate adjective ending

▶ using the superlative by adding *-(e)st* to the adjective as well as the appropriate ending and not forgetting the definite article *der, die* or *das*

▶ using irregular comparisons like *besser* and *höher* or irregular superlatives like *(das) beste* and *(das) nächste.*

(1) Translate into English:

1 Man muss kälteres Wasser in der Waschmaschine benutzen.
2 Die Ausbeutung der Wälder zeigt keinen Respekt für die Natur.
3 Das nächste Mal erwarten wir etwas Besseres!
4 Kohlendioxid hat die schlimmste Auswirkung auf unserer Atmosphäre.
5 Wir haben keine realistischeren Lösungen.
6 Was muss man machen, um den richtigen Weg zu finden?
7 Die Transportsysteme der Zukunft werden viel effizienter sein.
8 Eine reichhaltige Diät ist besser für die Gesundheit.
9 Klar bin ich viel optimistischer als du!
10 Die Sonne ist eine direkte Quelle von Licht und Wärme.

Translate into German:

11 Trains are more environmentally friendly than cars.
12 We have enough gas, but no petrol.
13 An old car is not good for the environment.
14 A new car is just as bad as an old one.
15 Their house has solar panels.
16 My central heating is expensive.
17 There's a good atmosphere in the eco-village.
18 People there live more cheaply than we do.
19 Do you recycle old newspapers and empty bottles?
20 Which energy is the cheapest?

Grammar

Revision of AS Grammar: pronouns

Check the grammar section of *Zeitgeist 2* and/or the Grammar Workbook if you need to know more about any of these things:

▸ direct object pronouns: *mich, dich, sich, uns, euch, ihnen*
▸ indirect object pronouns: *mir, dir, sich*
▸ reflexive pronouns used with reflexive verbs: *mich, dich, sich, uns, euch*
▸ the relative pronouns *der, die, das, dessen, deren*
▸ indefinite pronouns *jemand, niemand, jeder.*

(2) Translate into English:

1 Immigranten? Bezahlt man ihnen Kindergeld?
2 Laut des deutschen Grundgesetzes darf niemand wegen seiner Rasse benachteiligt werden.
3 Immigranten sind mit ihren Familien nach Deutschland gekommen.
4 In den letzten hundert Jahren haben deutsche Aussiedler wegen ihrer Nationalität viel gelitten.
5 Jeder hat das Recht auf die Nationalität vom Land seiner Geburt.
6 Immigranten sind zum Arbeiten in unser Land gekommen.
7 Wir sind gegen jeden, der die Menschenrechte nicht respektiert.
8 Deutschland ist das Land, in dem ich aufgewachsen bin und dessen Kultur ich mich anzupassen versuche.
9 Man erlaubt mir nicht, meine Herkunft zu vergessen.
10 Man wird nirgendwo als zugehörig betrachtet.

Translate into German:

11 Explain racism to me.
12 I told them I do not understand them.
13 He lives in Leipzig now and finds it very peaceful.
14 It is a town that I don't know.
15 Guest workers are mainly Turks, who came to Germany for work.
16 The resettlers are Germans who now live in Eastern Europe.
17 They have lived there for 20 years.
18 The map? Show me it, please.
19 Xenophobia – what is the cause?
20 We must try to replace it with tolerance.

Revision of AS Grammar: infinitives and the present tense

Check the grammar section of *Zeitgeist 2* and/or the Grammar Workbook if you need to know more about any of these things:

- ▶ the use of the infinitive construction with *zu*
- ▶ the use of modal verbs plus the infinitive
- ▶ the infinitive with *um ... zu*
- ▶ the present tense of regular verbs such as *wohnen, leben, arbeiten*
- ▶ the present tense of the modal verbs *wollen, sollen, dürfen, mögen*
- ▶ the present tense of irregular verbs such as *gehen, fahren, haben, sein, werden*
- ▶ the use of the present tense with *seit*
- ▶ the use of some verbs which take the dative such as *helfen, geben*.

(3) **Translate into English:**

1 Wie sind diese Probleme zu lösen?
2 Machen Sie schon etwas, um Geld für eine Wohlfahrtsorganisation aufzubringen?
3 Was brauchen solche Wohlfahrtsorganisationen, um funktionieren zu können?
4 Wir müssen eine langfristige Lösung finden.
5 Ohne Job kann man die Miete nicht bezahlen.
6 Ohne Unterkunft ist es schwierig, einen Job zu finden.
7 Wir versuchen, diesen Leuten zu helfen, ihre Gesellschaft wieder aufzubauen.
8 Den Entwicklungsländern sollte erlaubt sein, ihre Schulden bei den Industrieländern zu vergessen.
9 Wir dürfen nicht vergessen, dass alle Menschen Hilfe brauchen.
10 Wenn man in absoluter Armut lebt, hat man nicht genug zu essen.

Translate into German:

11 Everyone should have a certain standard of living.
12 Do you work for a charity?
13 I want to help people to have a future.
14 In many countries, lots of people cannot write or read.
15 I hope to be able to help them.
16 She wants to go to Africa to help the children there.
17 We have been working there for ten years.
18 Life can be very difficult for single mothers.
19 Lots of young people want to be rich.
20 What do you do if you can't find a job?

Revision of AS Grammar: past tenses

Check the grammar section of *Zeitgeist 2* and/or the Grammar Workbook if you need to know more about any of these things:

▸ the perfect tense with *haben*: *ich habe ... gemacht, ich habe ... gespielt*
▸ the perfect tense with *sein*: *ich bin ... gegangen, ich bin ... gefahren*
▸ the perfect tense of irregular verbs: *ich habe gesehen, ich habe gegessen*
▸ the perfect tense of separable verbs: *ich bin ... abgefahren, ich habe ... festgestellt*
▸ the imperfect tense: *er stand, ich sah, wir gingen*
▸ the pluperfect tense: *er hatte ... gesehen, ich war ... gegangen*
▸ the perfect tense of the passive voice: *es wurde verkauft.*

(4) Translate into English:

1 Der Dichter Johann Wolfgang von Goethe wurde 1749 geboren.
2 Karl Wilhelm Gropius hat eine Ausbildung als Landschaftsmaler in Berlin gemacht.
3 In dieser Zeit wurde die Gesellschaft von Männern beherrscht.
4 Fassbinder wurde 1945 geboren und verbrachte seine Kindheit in einem chaotischen Nachkriegsdeutschland
5 Marlene Dietrich ist in Berlin und Dessau zur Schule gegangen.
6 Im April 1930 hat sie Deutschland verlassen und ist nach Amerika ausgewandert.
7 Roland Emmerich begann seine Karriere als Regisseur in Deutschland.
8 Später hat er Ruhm in Amerika gefunden.
9 Der erste erfolgreiche Film von Wim Wenders war ‚Paris, Texas' (1984).
10 Sein Film ‚Der Himmel über Berlin' (1987) hat den Film ‚Stadt der Engel' (1998) mit Meg Ryan und Nicholas Cage inspiriert.

Translate into German:

11 How many people visited the Pergamon Museum in 2007?
12 This painting was sold for $78,000,000 last year.
13 Christa Wolf was born in 1929.
14 She did not believe in the dismantling of the GDR state.
15 At first, Lessing studied medicine and theology in Leipizig.
16 Later, he lived as a writer in Berlin, where he wrote for several newspapers.
17 In 1995, Franka Potente won the Bavarian Film Prize for Young Talent.
18 Tom Tykwer wrote the role of Lola in the film "Run, Lola, Run" for her.
19 Franka Potente has also written a screenplay.
20 Annette von Droste-Hülshoff wrote beautiful ballads and poems about Westphalia.

Revision of AS Grammar: future and conditional

Check the grammar section of *Zeitgeist 2* and/or the Grammar Workbook if you need to know more about any of these things:

▸ using the present tense to refer to things which are going to happen soon, with mention of a future time: *Morgen gehe ich ins Kino, nächste Woche bleiben wir hier.*

▸ using *werden* + infinitive to refer to precise future plans: *ich werde ... wohnen, wir werden ... sehen*

▸ using *ich möchte* + infinitive to describe something that you would like to happen: *ich möchte ... arbeiten*

▸ forming the conditional tense using imperfect subjunctive of *werden* + infinitive to say what would happen in certain circumstances: *wir würden ... verbringen*

▸ using *wenn* with the conditional/imperfect subjunctive. (NB: unlike English, the same tense must be used in both parts of the sentence)

▸ forming the imperfect subjunctive: *ich wäre, ich hätte, ich ginge, ich käme.*

(5) Translate into English:

1 Morgen werden wir in einer Welt voller Computer leben.
2 In der Zukunft werden Computer Ihnen helfen, alles zu erledigen.
3 Es wird nicht mehr nötig sein, aus dem Hause zu gehen, weil man zu Hause alles haben wird, was man braucht.
4 Die Entscheidungen der Wissenschaftler werden ernste Folgen haben.
5 Aufgrund der Gentechnik wird es möglich sein, viele Erbkrankheiten zu heilen.
6 Aber in den nächsten fünf Jahren wird es keine Wunderheilmittel geben.
7 Das Manipulieren von menschlichem Erbgut könnte eine Welt voller perfekter Menschen schaffen.
8 Alle Lebensmittel werden gentechnisch verändert werden.
9 Gentechnisch veränderte Lebensmittel könnten neue Allergien verursachen.
10 Wenn man wüsste, dass solche Lebensmittel unschädlich wären, könnte man damit die Ernährungsprobleme in den Entwicklungsländern lösen.

Translate into German:

11 How will we live in the future?
12 There will be computers everywhere.
13 We will do our shopping on the Internet.
14 You'll be able to spend your holiday on the moon.
15 What will daily life be like?
16 My computer will help me make decisions.
17 Scientists will have to be very responsible.
18 I would not like to live in a perfect world.
19 People should know more about technology.
20 If I were young, I would study I.T.

Revision of AS Grammar: negatives

Check the grammar section of *Zeitgeist 2* and/or the Grammar Workbook if you need to know more about any of these things:

▶ using *nicht and nie* to negate a verb, remembering to place it near the end of the sentence
▶ using *nicht* to precede words for emphasis
▶ using indefinite pronouns: *nirgendwo, niemand*
▶ using *kein* as a negative with nouns: *keine Ahnung*
▶ using *weder ... noch* to give two balanced negatives
▶ using *nicht nur ... sondern auch* to translate 'not only ... but also'
▶ using *nichts*.

6 Translate into English:

1 Wir dürfen nicht vergessen, dass die kulturelle Vielfalt in Europa sehr wichtig ist.
2 Haben Sie keine Angst vor der EU!
3 Im Moment hat die EU weder einen Präsidenten noch Soldaten.
4 Wir waren noch nie in Frankreich.
5 Ich habe keine Angst, meine Identität zu verlieren.
6 Alte Menschen werden nicht mehr isoliert, sondern respektiert und geschätzt sein.
7 Die EU hat nicht nur für die Zukunft gute Ideen, sondern auch konkrete Vorschläge, wie man diese Ideen finanzieren kann.
8 Europa hat nichts zu verbergen.
9 Nicht alle EU-Mitglieder wollen den Euro.
10 Die globale Wirtschaft hat kein Vertrauen in die europäischen Politiker.

Translate into German:

11 Isn't Poland a member of the EU?
12 He had not voted.
13 You will never visit Russia.
14 The EU is no longer small.
15 I would not like to be the EU President!
16 I no longer have a passport.
17 Nothing is more certain.
18 I have not a single euro left.
19 I prefer not to take my holidays in Europe.
20 I have neither the time nor the money.

Revision of AS Grammar: word order

Word order is very important in German. You must remember the rules:

▸ the main verb is always the second idea
▸ the order of adverbs is time – manner – place
▸ conjunctions can change the word order: *weil, wenn* and *dass* send the verb to the end of the clause
▸ if a sentence begins with a subordinate clause, the subject and verb in the main clause invert to form "a verb sandwich"
▸ in relative clauses, the verb goes to the end of the clause (NB: relative pronouns must be used in German).

(7) Translate into English:

1 Natürlich hat sie sich sehr gefreut, als sie gute Noten bekommen hat.
2 Viele Frauen entscheiden sich für Teilzeitarbeit, wenn sie Kinder haben.
3 Er hat nicht viel in der Schule gearbeitet, aber jetzt arbeitet er fleißig in der Lehre.
4 Sie studiert in Deutschland, weil sie sehr gut Deutsch sprechen kann.
5 Da sie in einer Bank arbeiten will, hofft sie, Mathe an der Universität zu studieren.
6 Marlene Dietrich ist nach Amerika ausgewandert, weil sie die Nazis hasste.
7 ‚Lola rennt' ist die Geschichte einer Frau, die ihren Freund retten will.
8 Berlin ist eine schöne Stadt mit viel Geschichte.
9 Da man in der Schweiz verschiedene Sprachen spricht, ist es ein kompliziertes Land.
10 Brandenburg ist eines der neuen Bundesländer, die früher ein Teil der DDR waren.

Translate into German:

11 Last year, I studied at Bremen University.
12 Many young people speak foreign languages very well and therefore can find work anywhere in the EU.
13 She was not interested in big films but wanted to tell unusual stories.
14 Anne Frank liked it very much when people visited her.
15 The Stasi time was very difficult because you distrusted everyone.
16 The Nazi time was just as bad, as everyone was afraid.
17 As West Berliners could no longer go to East Berlin, many people could not go to work.
18 The wall was built because many East Germans wanted to leave the country.
19 West Berlin was very isolated because there was only one road in.
20 Marlene Dietrich was born in Berlin in 1901.

Grammar

A2 Grammar: the subjunctive

What you need to know

As well as an alternative to the conditional, the subjunctive in German in used for direct or reported speech. The present and perfect subjunctive are the most useful here:

To form the present subjunctive, add the following endings to the stem of the verb:

ich -e, du -est, er/sie -e, wir -en, ihr -et, sie -en.

The exception to this is *sein:*

ich sei, du seiest, er sei, wir seien, ihr seiet, sie seien.

The perfect subjunctive is formed quite logically with the present subjunctive of the auxiliary *haben* or *sein* plus the past participle: *ich sei gegangen, ich habe gemacht.*

The imperfect subjunctive is often used for politeness, expressing wishes and requests:

ich hätte gern ..., ich möchte ...

The imperfect and pluperfect subjunctives are frequently used after conjunctions such as *als* and *als ob.*

The future subjunctive is formed by using the present subjunctive of *werden* plus the infinitive.

(8) Translate into English:

1 Die Studenten erklärten, sie seien immer sehr spät ins Bett gegangen.
2 Meine Freundin fragte mich, ob ich Fremdsprachen studieren wolle.
3 Er hat immer gesagt, dass ihm seine Arbeit gefalle.
4 Sie sagte, sie habe zu viel zu tun.
5 Ich möchte ein gutes Zeugnis haben.
6 Es sieht nicht so aus, als ob er Arbeit finden würde.
7 Sie tut nicht so, als wäre sie fleißig.
8 Würden Sie bitte hier unterschreiben?
9 Ich hätte gern einen guten Job.
10 Sie sagten, sie hätten nichts geplant.

Translate into German:

11 I would like to study in Germany.
12 She said that she was happy.
13 They acted as though they loved German.
14 He said the film was really good.
15 They said they saw a wonderful play last week.
16 Would you please sit down?
17 She looked as though she was tired.
18 I said I did not want to work every day.
19 She asked why we did not come to the party.
20 It isn't as if she went out every night.

A2 Grammar: the passive

What you need to know

At A2 Level, you are expected to be familiar with the use of the passive tenses:

▶ the present passive: *es wird gemacht* = it is being done

▶ the imperfect passive: *es wurde gemacht* = it was being done

▶ the perfect passive: *es ist gemacht worden* = it has been done

▶ the pluperfect passive: *es war gemacht worden* = it had been done

▶ the future passive: *es wird gemacht werden* = it will be done

NB: with modal verbs, the tense is expressed through the modal verb, and the other verb remains in the passive infinitive: *es muss sofort gemacht werden.*

(9) Translate into English:

1 Es wurde ihnen gesagt, dass man schnell etwas tun solle.
2 In der Umweltpolitik wird nicht genug getan.
3 Abwässer von Chemiefabriken wurden oft in den Rhein geleitet.
4 Atomkraft wird in vielen Kraftwerken produziert.
5 Plastiktüten werden mehrmals verwendet.
6 Plastikflaschen wurden durch Glasflaschen ersetzt.
7 Sperrmüll wurde regelmäßig abgeholt.
8 Abfallsünder wurden bestraft.
9 Katalysatoren mussten in Autos eingebaut werden.
10 In vielen Gärten sind Komposthaufen schon angelegt worden.

Translate into German:

11 It will never be done.
12 Glass and metal were collected separately.
13 Pictures of rubbish heaps and the hole in the ozone layer are being shown.
14 Old paper had been collected.
15 Competitions with prizes were organised.
16 Wonderful cloth bags have been produced.
17 The shopping ought to be put in them.
18 The bus has been used more often.
19 The bike cannot be used at the moment.
20 It was damaged in an accident last week.

Pronunciation

b, d und g

CD Track 4

Vergleichen Sie:

Bild	o**b**
blei**b**en	schrei**b**t
Deutsch	gesun**d**
dürfen	bal**d**
gut	Ta**g**
ganz	Erfol**g**

Consonants **b**, **d** and **g** are pronounced like **p**, **t** and **k** respectively when they appear at the end of a word or in front of **s** or **t**.

Üben Sie jetzt diese Sätze:

Jeden Tag gesund essen – der gute Weg zum Erfolg!
Mein deutscher Freund wird bald kommen.
Ich weiß nicht, ob er lange bleibt.

-ig, -ich, -isch

CD Track 5

Wiederholen Sie die Adjektive:

wen**ig**	mög**lich**	prak**tisch**
bill**ig**	eigent**lich**	poli**tisch**
witz**ig**	jugend**lich**	laun**isch**
güns**tig**	schrift**lich**	erfinder**isch**

Versuchen Sie jetzt diesen Zungenbrecher:

Theoretisch ist das richtig, aber eigentlich gar nicht wichtig – beschwichtigt der ewig praktische Herr Derwisch.

s, ß, st, sp

CD Track 6

Üben Sie diese Wörter:

Sonntag	*sein*
Stein	*Straße*
Fußball	*Spaß*
Sorge	*Pass*
Staatsangehörigkeit	*Statistik*

Zungenbrecher:

Am Sonntag sitzt sein Sohn auf der Straße in der Stadt, sonst strickt er Socken, spielt Fußball und sammelt Steine.

ei, ie

CD Track 7

Wiederholen Sie:

eins, zwei, drei
Eintracht und Zwietracht
Dienstag, Mittwoch und Freitag
schwierig
der Schweiß

Die Arbeit ist nicht schwierig, aber schweißtreibend.
Ich schreibe. Ich schrieb. Ich habe geschrieben.
Er muss sich entscheiden. Er hat sich entschieden.
Liebeslieder von Liebe und Leiden

Lange und kurze Vokale

CD Track 8

Wiederholen Sie:

langer Vokal:
 mag, Rad, Spaß, Abend, sagen
 sehr, gehen, jedes, Federball, Meter
 mir, hier, Spiel, Ziel, viel
 ohne, wohnen, so, oder, Mode
 Ruhe, Schule, Fuß, zu, nun

kurzer Vokal:
 hallo, etwas, Geschmack, Stadt, satt
 Essen, Tennis, schlecht, Welt, Geld
 bist, sich, immer, finden, Wirkung
 kommen, besonders, Kosten, gebrochen, noch
 muss, Mutter, Eiskunstlauf, Druck, Schuss

Vokale mit Umlaut

CD Track 9

Wiederholen Sie:

schön	*erhöht*	*gewöhnlich*	*könnte*
über	*hübsch*	*Grüße*	*müsste*
Ähnlichkeit	*erwähnen*	*Fähigkeit*	*ändern*

Lesen Sie diese Wörter laut. Überprüfen Sie danach die Aussprache.

übertrieben	*Aufklärungsarbeit*	*hören*	*jeder fünfte*	*Gegensätze*
möglich	*Gefühl*	*Schönheitsideal*	*schädlich*	*fünf*
Essstörungen	*gefährlich*	*Öffentlichkeit*	*übermäßig*	*abhängig*

Zungenbrecher:

Der Mondschein schien schon schön.

Pronunciation

-z und -zw

CD Track 10

Wiederholen Sie:

Ziel	Zug	Zaun	Zweig	Zwerg	Zweck
Einzelzimmer	jetzt	zuletzt	kurz	nützlich	
Unterstützung	Sturz	Arzt	zwanzig	gezwungen	zwölf

Hören Sie zu und wiederholen Sie:

jetzt – zuletzt
zu zweit – Zeit
kurz – Sturz
zwanzig – Zwetschgen
Zweck – Zecke

Probieren Sie diese Sätze:

Setzen Sie sich in den Zug.
Zwischen zwölf und zwei.
Zieh jetzt kurz am Seil.
Zwei Ziegen sitzen vor dem Zaun.

Zungenbrecher:

Zwischen zwei Zelten zwitschern zwölf Zaunkönige.

Compound words

CD Track 11

Wiederholen Sie:

a Gleich/geschlechtliche Partnerschaften
b Lebens/abschnitts/gefährte
c Wieder/heirat
d Geschäfts/reise
e auseinander/brechen
f Kinder/tages/stätte
g Wieder/vereinigung
h Gehirn/masse
i Wohn/gemeinschaft
j Abenteuer/lust

Unit 1: Umweltverschmutzung und Energieverbrauch

die Umwelt	the environment
der Umweltschutz	environmental conservation
der Treibhauseffekt	greenhouse effect
die Energiekrise	the energy crisis
der Energiebedarf	energy need
der Sonnenkollektor(-en)	a solar panel
die Sonnenenergie/der Solarstrom	solar energy
die Energiequelle	source of energy
das Windrad	wind turbine
die Atomenergie	nuclear power
das Kernkraftwerk	nuclear power station
belasten	to pollute
verpesten	to pollute
schaden	to damage
verschwenden	to waste
vergiften	to poison
gefährden	to endanger
erschöpft werden	to run out
die Entwaldung	deforestation
die Erwärmung der Erdatmosphäre	global warming
die Überschwemmung	flood
der Orkan(-e)	hurricane
schmelzen	to melt
der Säuregehalt	level of acidity
der Meeresspiegel	ocean level
die Ursache	cause
die Auswirkung	effect
der Klimawandel	climate change
der Gletscher	glacier

Unit 2: Umweltschutz

umweltfreundlich	environmentally friendly
umweltfeindlich	damaging to the environment
schützen	to protect
das Umweltbewusstsein	environmental awareness
die Umwelterziehung	environmental education
die Schadstoffbelastung mindern	to reduce damage by pollutants
retten	to save
die Bedrohung der Menschen	threat to humanity
die dauerhafte Entwicklung	sustainable development
demonstrieren/eine Demonstration	to demonstrate/a demonstration
verbessern	to improve
das Benehmen ändern	to change the behaviour

Vocabulary

die Ausstellung	exhibition
kämpfen gegen	to fight against
der Gegner	activists
das Licht ausschalten	to put out the light
die Heizung herunterdrehen	to turn down the heating
die Fahrgemeinschaft	car-sharing
Müll trennen	(to separate) household rubbish
der Sperrmüll	bulky rubbish
recyceln/das Recycling	to recycle/recycling
die Industrieländer	the industrialised countries
alternative Energiequellen	alternative energy sources
entwickeln	to develop
die Plastiktüte	plastic bag
biologisch abbaubar	biodegradable
vernichten	to destroy
das Benzin	petrol
das Rohöl	crude oil
die Kohle	coal
der Energieverbrauch	energy consumption
der Brennstoff	fuel
der Wasserstoff	hydrogen
der Sauerstoff	oxygen
das Kohlendioxid	carbon dioxide CO_2

Unit 3: Ausländer

der Ausländer	foreigner
der Aussiedler	resettler
der Gastarbeiter	guest worker
der Asylbewerber	asylum seeker
das Herkunftsland	country of origin
der Einwanderer	immigrant
der Auswanderer	emigrant
der Antrag	application
verfolgt	persecuted
integrieren	integrate
der Bürger	citizen
die Einbürgerung	citizenship
die Aufenthaltserlaubnis	residence permit
die Arbeitsgenehmigung	work permit
die Familie nachholen	to bring one's family over
sich einleben	to settle down
unqualifizierte Arbeit	unskilled work
schlecht bezahlt	poorly paid
niedrig	menial

ablehnen	to reject
die kulturelle Indentität wahren	to maintain cultural identity
Anst haben (vor)	to be afraid
die Ungleichheit	inequality
der Rassismus	racism
die Rassendiskriminierung	racial discrimination
die Ausländerfeindlichkeit	xenophobia, dislike of foreigners
der Neonazismus	neo-Nazism
der kulturelle Konflikt	cultural clash
verschlimmern/verbessern	to get worse/to improve
der Sündenbock	scapegoat
die Rassenkonflikte	racial tensions
die Gewalt	violence
die Rassenunruhen	riots
die Feindseligkeit	hostility
fremd	foreign
der gegenseitige Respekt	mutual respect
die Toleranz	tolerance
die kulturelle Vielfalt	cultural diversity
zweisprachig	bilingual

Unit 4: Armut und Reichtum

die Armut	poverty
das Elend	misery
die Armutsgrenze	poverty threshold
die Kluft	gap
der Reichtum	riches
der Obdachlose	homeless person
obdachlos	homeless
arbeitslos/die Arbeitslosigkeit	unemployed/unemployment
betteln	to beg
der Bettler	beggar
die Herberge	hostel
die Dritte Welt	the Third World
die Sozialhilfe	social services
die Entwicklungsländer	developing countries
die Unterernährung	malnutrition
die Hungersnot	famine
die Dürre	drought
die Infektionskrankheiten	infectious diseases
der Krieg	war
die Katastrophe	disaster
das Erdbeben	earthquake
die medizinische Fürsorge	medical/health care

Vocabulary

teilen	to share
Probleme lösen	to solve problems
die Ausbildung anregen	to encourage schooling
fairer Handel	fair trade
von seiner Arbeit leben	to live from one's work
die Ausbeutung	exploitation
die Biobaumwolle	organic cotton
das anständige Gehalt	fair pay
die Gleichberechtigung	equality
das Wohlwollen	goodwill
die Grundrechte	basic rights
die moralischen Werte	ethical values
der Wohlfahrtsverband	charity
fördern	(to) support
freiwillig	voluntary

Unit 5: Rechtswesen und Verbrechen

die Gewalt	violence
tatverdächtig sein	to be suspected (of a crime)
das Delikt(e)	crime
verurteilt	convicted
der Straftäter	criminal
die Straftat	crime
der Ladendiebstahl	shoplifting
die Sachbeschädigung	criminal damage
Schwarzfahren	fare dodging
die Körperverletzung	physical injury
anzeigen	to press charges
begehen	commit
benachrichtigen	to report
das Verbrechen	crime
der Diebstahl	theft
die Gewalttat	crime of violence
das Gerichtsverfahren	court hearing
der Betrug	fraud, scam
das Betäubungsmittel	narcotic
die Strafverfolgungsbehörde	law enforcement agency
erforderlich	necessary, essential
verführen	to seduce
verboten	forbidden
illegal	illegal
vorsichtig	careful
misstrauisch	suspicious

verlockend	alluring, tempting
die Gefängnisstrafe	prison sentence
das Gefängnis	prison
die Todesstrafe	death penalty
die Abschreckung	deterrent
das Opfer	victim
die Überwachungskamera	security camera

Unit 6: Technik und die Zukunft

die neue Technologie	new technology
genetisch	genetic
die Gentechnik	genetic engineering
das Klonen/klonen	cloning/to clone
entdecken	to discover
gentechnisch verändert	genetically modified
genmanipuliert	genetically modified
das Erbgut	genetic make-up
das Gen	gene
erfinden/die Erfindung	to invent/invention
die Zeitreise	time travel
die Reise begrenzen	to limit the journey
im Internet einkaufen	to shop on the Internet
der Fortschritt	progress
ein defektes Gen	a defective gene
eine erblich bedingte Fehlsteuerung	a congenital disorder
die Erbkrankheit	hereditary illness
heilen	to cure
ethische Bedenken	ethical considerations
die Transplantation	transplant
das Retortenbaby	test-tube baby
der Embryo	embryo
der DNS-Code	DNA code
der Spender	donor
die Lebensqualität	quality of life
verbessern	to improve
entwickeln	to develop
Wirklichkeit werden	to become reality
forschen über	to research into
die Forschung	research
das Reagenzglas	test tube
die embryonale Stammzelle	embryonic stem cell
ausgestorben	extinct

Vocabulary

Unit 7: Literatur, Film und die schönen Künste

die Schönheit	beauty
die Wahrheit	truth
der Geschmack	taste
schildern	to depict
der Leser	the reader
eine Geschichte erzählen	to tell a story
in anderen Sprachen übersetzt	translated into other languages
das Drehbuch	screenplay
einen Film drehen	to make a film
der Handwerker	craftsman
der Dichter	poet
das Gedicht	poem
der Regisseur	director
der Roman	novel
der Künstler	artist
der Schriftsteller	writer
das Stück	play
der Titel	title
düster	bleak
die Hauptfigur	main character
die Regie	direction
die Anerkennung	recognition
der Kassenerfolg	box-office success
die Kritik	review
der Schauplatz	scene
der Schauspieler	actor
der Hauptdarsteller	principal actor
die Landschaft	landscape
das Mitglied	member
entdeckt	discovered
der Schwarzmarkt	black market
der Maler	painter
das Motiv	theme
das Werk	work
zu Lebzeiten	when alive
das Gemälde	painting
der Architekt	architect

Unit 8: Deutschland heute

die Mauer	wall
die Teilung	separation
die Wende	turning point

die Wiedervereinigung	reunification
Ossis	people from East Germany
Wessis	people from West Germany
die EU	European Union
der Euro	euro
die Muttersprache	mother tongue
die Wirtschaft	economy
das Wirtschaftswachstum	economic growth
das Zusammengehörigkeitsgefühl	feeling of belonging
die Mitgliedstaaten (pl)	member states
deutschsprachig	German speaking

Unit 9: Die Politik und globale Probleme

die Globalisierung	globalisation
die Regierung	government
der Staat	state
die Wirtschaftsmacht	economic power
der Weltmarkt	world market
wettbewerbsfähig	competitive
die Demokratie	democracy
die Macht	power
das Recht	the right
versammeln	to assemble, congregate
rechtsextremistisch	right-wing
der Krieg	war
der Frieden	peace
beherrschen	rule
der Angriff	attack
der Drahtzieher	manipulator
der Attentäter	assassin
der Terrorverdächtige	terrorist suspect
vereitelt	thwarted
der Bundestag	German parliament
der Eiserne Vorhang	Iron Curtain
die Ölkrise	oil crisis
der Abbau	phasing out
Terrorismus bekämpfen	to combat terrorism
stimmen für/gegen	to vote for/against
die Wahl	election
die Stimme	the vote

Grammar answers

1 We must use cooler water in the washing machine.
2 Forest exploitation shows no respect for nature.
3 We expect better next time!
4 Carbon dioxide has the worst effect on our atmosphere.
5 We have no more realistic solutions.
6 What should we do to find the right road?
7 The transport system of the future will be much more efficient.
8 A varied diet is better for health.
9 I am clearly more optimistic than you are.
10 The sun is a direct source of light and heat.
11 Züge sind umweltfreundlicher als Autos.
12 Wir haben genug Erdgas, aber kein Benzin.
13 Ein altes Auto ist nicht gut für die Umwelt.
14 Ein neues Auto ist genauso schlimm wie ein altes.
15 Ihr Haus hat Sonnenkollektoren.
16 Meine Zentralheizung ist teuer.
17 Es gibt eine gute Atmosphäre im Ökodorf.
18 Dort wohnen die Leute billiger als bei uns.
19 Recyceln Sie (Recycelst du) alte Zeitungen und leere Flaschen?
20 Welche Energie ist am billigsten?

1 Immigrants? Do we pay them child benefit?
2 According to German law, no one can be disadvantaged because of their race.
3 Immigrants came to Germany with their families.
4 In the last hundred years, German re-settlers have suffered much because of their nationality.
5 We all have the right to the nationality of the country in which we are born.
6 Immigrants came to work in our country.
7 We stand against anyone who doesn't respect human rights.
8 Germany is the country in which I grew up and whose culture I try to adapt to.
9 I am not allowed to forget my origins.
10 We are regarded as belonging to nowhere.
11 Erklären Sie (Erkläre) mir, was Rassismus bedeutet.
12 Ich habe ihnen gesagt, dass ich sie nicht verstehe.
13 Er wohnt jetzt in Leipzig und findet die Stadt sehr ruhig.
14 Das ist eine Stadt, die ich nicht kenne.
15 Gastarbeiter sind hauptsächlichTürken, die zum Arbeiten nach Deutschland gekommen sind.
16 Die Aussiedler sind Deutsche, die jetzt in Osteuropa wohnen.
17 Sie wohnen dort seit 20 Jahren.
18 Die Karte? Zeigen Sie (Zeig) sie mir, bitte.

19 Die Ausländerfeindlichkeit – was ist die Ursache davon?
20 Wir müssen versuchen, sie mit Toleranz zu ersetzen.

1 How do you solve these problems?
2 Do you already do something to raise money for a charity?
3 What do such charities need in order to be able to function?
4 We must find a long-term solution.
5 Without a job, you cannot pay the rent.
6 Without accommodation it is difficult to find a job
7 We try to help these people to rebuild their society.
8 The Third World countries should be allowed to forget their debts to the industrial countries.
9 We must not forget that all people need help.
10 When you live in absolute poverty, you do not have enough to eat.
11 Jeder sollte einen bestimmten Lebensstandard haben.
12 Arbeitest du/Arbeiten Sie bei einer Wohlfahrtsorganisation?
13 Ich will anderen Leuten helfen, eine Zukunft zu haben.
14 In vielen Ländern können viele Leute weder schreiben noch lesen.
15 Ich hoffe, ihnen helfen zu können.
16 Sie will nach Afrika gehen, um dort den Kindern zu helfen.
17 Wir arbeiten dort schon seit zehn Jahren.
18 Das Leben kann für allein erziehende Mütter sehr schwierig sein.
19 Viele junge Leute wollen reich sein.
20 Was macht man, wenn man keinen Job finden kann?

1 The poet Johann Wolfgang von Goethe was born in 1749.
2 Karl Wilhelm Gropius trained as a landscape painter in Berlin.
3 In this era, society was dominated by men.
4 Fassbinder was born in 1945 and spent his childhood in a chaotic post-war Germany.
5 Marlene Dietrich went to school in Berlin and Dessau.
6 In April 1930, she left Germany and emigrated to America.
7 Roland Emmerich began his career as a film director in Germany.
8 Later he found fame in America.
9 Wim Wenders' first successful film was 'Paris, Texas' (1984).
10 His 1987 film 'Wings of Desire' inspired the 1998 film 'City of Angels' with Meg Ryan and Nicholas Cage.
11 Wie viele Leute haben das Pergamonmuseum im Jahr 2007 besucht?
12 Letztes Jahr wurde dieses Bild für $78 000 000 verkauft.
13 Christa Wolf wurde 1929 geboren.
14 Sie glaubte nicht an die Auflösung der DDR.
15 Lessing studierte zuerst Medizin und Theologie in Leipzig.
16 Danach lebte er als Schriftsteller in Berlin, wo er für mehrere Zeitungen schrieb.

17 1995 gewann Franka Potente den Bayerischen Filmpreis als beste Nachwuchsschauspielerin.

18 Tom Tykwer schrieb die Rolle der Lola im Film ‚Lola rennt' für sie.

19 Franka Potente hat auch ein Drehbuch geschrieben.

20 Annette von Droste-Hülshoff schrieb schöne Balladen und Gedichte über Westfalen.

1 Tomorrow we will live in a world full of computers.

2 In the future, computers will help you get everything done.

3 It will no longer be necessary to leave the house, for you will have everything you need at home.

4 Scientists' decisions will have serious consequences.

5 Because of genetics, it will be possible to cure many hereditary illnesses.

6 But there will be no miracle cure in the next five years.

7 Genetic manipulation could create a world full of perfect people.

8 All food will be genetically modified.

9 Genetically modified food could cause new allergies.

10 If you knew that such food was harmless, you could solve the food problems of the developing countries with it.

11 Wie werden wir in der Zukunft leben?

12 Es wird überall Computer geben.

13 Wir werden im Internet einkaufen.

14 Man wird seinen Urlaub auf dem Mond verbringen können.

15 Wie wird das tägliche Leben aussehen?

16 Mein Computer wird mir helfen, Entscheidungen zu treffen.

17 Die Wissenschaftler werden sehr verantwortungsvoll sein müssen.

18 Ich möchte nicht in einer perfekten Welt wohnen.

19 Man sollte mehr über Technologie wissen.

20 Wenn ich jung wäre, würde ich Informatik studieren.

1 We must not forget that cultural diversity is very important in Europe.

2 Don't be afraid of the European Union!

3 For the moment, the EU has neither president nor soldiers.

4 We have never been to France.

5 I am not afraid of losing my identity.

6 Old people will no longer be isolated but respected and valued.

7 Not only has the EU good ideas for the future but also concrete proposals to finance these ideas.

8 Europe has nothing to hide.

9 Not all EU members want the euro.

10 The global economy has no confidence in the European politicians.

11 Ist Polen kein EU-Mitglied?

12 Er hatte nicht gewählt.

13 Du wirst (Sie werden) Russland nie besuchen.
14 Die EU ist nicht mehr klein.
15 Ich möchte nicht EU-Präsident sein!
16 Ich habe keinen Pass mehr.
17 Nichts ist sicherer.
18 Ich habe keinen einzigen Euro übrig.
19 Ich verbringe meine Ferien lieber nicht in Europa.
20 Ich habe weder die Zeit noch das Geld.

7

1 Of course she was pleased when she got good marks.
2 Many women choose to work part-time when they have children.
3 He did not work much in school, but he works very hard now in his apprenticeship.
4 She is studying in Germany because she can speak German very well.
5 Because she wants to work in a bank, she hopes to study maths at university.
6 Marlene Dietrich emigrated to America because she hated the Nazis.
7 "Run, Lola, Run" is the story of a woman who wants to save her boyfriend.
8 Berlin is a beautiful city with lots of history.
9 Because they speak different languages in Switzerland, it is a complicated country.
10 Brandenburg is one of the new federal counties which used to be a part of the GDR.
11 Letztes Jahr habe ich an der Universität Bremen studiert.
12 Viele junge Leute sprechen sehr gut Fremdsprachen, und deshalb können sie überall in der EU einen Job finden.
13 Sie interessierte sich nicht für große Filme, sondern wollte außergewöhnliche Geschichten erzählen.
14 Es hat Anne Frank sehr gefallen, als Leute sie besucht haben.
15 Die Stasizeit war sehr schlimm, weil man jedem misstraute.
16 Die Nazizeit war genauso schlimm, da jeder Angst hatte.
17 Da die Westberliner nicht mehr nach Ostberlin durften, konnten viele Leute nicht zur Arbeit gehen.
18 Man hat die Mauer gebaut, weil viele Ostdeutschen das Land verlassen wollten.
19 Westberlin war sehr isoliert, weil es nur einen Einweg gab.
20 Marlene Dietrich wurde 1901 in Berlin geboren.

8

1 The students explained that they always went to bed very late.
2 My friend asked me if I wanted to study languages.
3 He always said he liked his work.

4 She said she had too much to do.
5 I would like a good report.
6 It does not look as though he will find work.
7 She does not act as if she were hardworking.
8 Would you please sign here?
9 I would like a good job.
10 They said they had nothing planned.
11 Ich möchte in Deutschland studieren.
12 Sie sagte, sie sei glücklich.
13 Sie benahmen sich, als ob sie Deutsch geliebt hätten.
14 Er sagte, der Film sei wirklich gut.
15 Sie sagten, letzte Woche hätten sie ein wunderbares Theaterstück gesehen.
16 Würden Sie sich bitte hinsetzen?
17 Sie sah aus, als ob sie müde wäre.
18 Ich sagte, ich wolle nicht jeden Tag arbeiten.
19 Sie fragte, warum wir nicht auf die Party kämen.
20 Es ist nicht so, als ob sie jeden Abend ausginge.

1 They were told that something should be done quickly.
2 Not enough is being done in environmental politics.
3 Effluents from chemical factories were often poured into the Rhine.
4 Nuclear power is produced in many power stations.
5 Plastic bags are used many times.
6 Plastic bottles were replaced by glass bottles.
7 Bulky rubbish was collected regularly.
8 Litterbugs were punished.
9 Catalytic converters had to be built into cards.
10 Compost heaps have already been set up in many gardens.
11 Es wird nie gemacht werden.
12 Glas und Metall wurden getrennt gesammelt.
13 Bilder von Müllbergen und vom Ozonloch werden gezeigt.
14 Altpapier war gesammelt worden.
15 Wettbewerbe mit Preisen wurden veranstaltet.
16 Wundervolle Stofftaschen sind hergestellt worden.
17 Die Einkäufe sollten dort hineingepackt werden.
18 Der Bus ist öfter benutzt worden.
19 Das Rad kann im Moment nicht benutzt werden.
20 Es wurde letzte Woche in einem Unfall beschädigt.